# The Bessbrook and Newry Tramway
## A.T. Newham

Car No. 1 at Bessbrook terminus, showing the detail of the pantograph.

*Oakwood collection*

View of the Bessbrook and Newry's track approaching the Great Northern Railway's Craigmore viaduct. The double rail, best seen on the left, allowed flangeless wagons to run on the line. The outer rail of the two was lower than the inner which acted as a guide for the wagon; the centre rail provided electricity for the cars. *H. Fayle*

© A.T. Newham, 1979
First published in the United Kingdom, 1979,
Reprinted in new format with minor corrections,
and additional photographs, 2020
by The Oakwood Press
54-58 Mill Square, Catrine, KA5 6RD

www.stenlake.co.uk
ISBN 978-0-85361-748-8

The publishers regret that they cannot supply
copies of any pictures featured in this book.

Printed by
P2D Books, 1 Newlands Rd, Westoning, Bedford MK45 5LD

## Acknowledgements

My thanks to the Librarian of the Institute of Civil Engineers, London, the Public Record Office, Belfast, for access to the only four available Minute Books of the tramway company, to Mr J.C. Gillham, London, for a map of the line and use of matter contained in a Paper which he compiled, to Mr M. Evans of South Croydon, for the use of extracts from Garcke's Manual, and similar data.

## Publisher's Note

Mr A. T. Newham was an indefatigable chronicler of the minor Irish railways and tramways. An illness in early youth left Mr Newham with the stature of a boy of 10, but he did not allow his tiny form to interfere with his hobby, and even fired on the footplate on occasion. As a friend of H. Fayle, whose 1946 work brought about the study of Irish light railways, Mr Newham was a link with the days when Ireland was a treasure chest for the railway enthusiast, and he was able to set these things down as he knew them and not as he read about them.

Tramway terminus at Bessbrook. *Oakwood Collection*

# Construction and Opening

The Bessbrook & Newry Tramway (B&N) was the second of the Irish narrow gauge (3 ft) lines to be operated on the hydro-electric principle. The first was the Giants Causeway Tramway. The Bessbrook & Newry, unlike the Giants Causeway Tramway, was unobtrusive and off the beaten track; the average tourist speeding north (until 1948) by rail over the 126-feet-high Craigmore viaduct en route for Belfast would hardly notice the narrow set of rails wending their way down the valley below. Its construction was inspired by Messrs Richardsons, well-known Quakers, who in 1846 acquired the Bessbrook Spinning Mills, founded near the end of the 18th century and much enlarged by them. They also built two large blocks of flats, a church, and an Institute at Bessbrook, making it a model village for their workers.

In those days road transport, all horse-drawn, was very slow, and the tramway was built with two objects: to provide a convenient means to transport coal and flax from the Newry Quays to the mills, and in the reverse direction finished goods such as linens, damask, towels and sheets; and also to provide transport for such workers as lived in Newry. According to a Provisional Order issued in 1881, it was originally intended to work the main tramway with steam or other motive power, and three lines were envisaged; the main line from Newry to Bessbrook, and two goods spurs:

1. a line commencing at Newry on the west side of the Albert Basin on the Carlingford Road, south of the Dublin drawbridge, and continuing via Butter Crane and Merchants Quay to a junction with Monaghan Street. Then north-west up this street to its junction with Edward Street, crossing the latter (a right turn) and on via the later route (but further north-west) to Craigmore, then west along the Camlough Stream and across the roadway to Millvale; then north and west to its Bessbrook terminus.
2. a spur continuing across the roadway on the level for 7 furlongs to a quarry.
3. at the Newry end, a spur off No. 1 north of the Dublin Drawbridge along the east side of the Albert Basin and ending near the Dundalk & Newry Steam Packet Company's warehouse. No. 3 was only to be worked by horses.

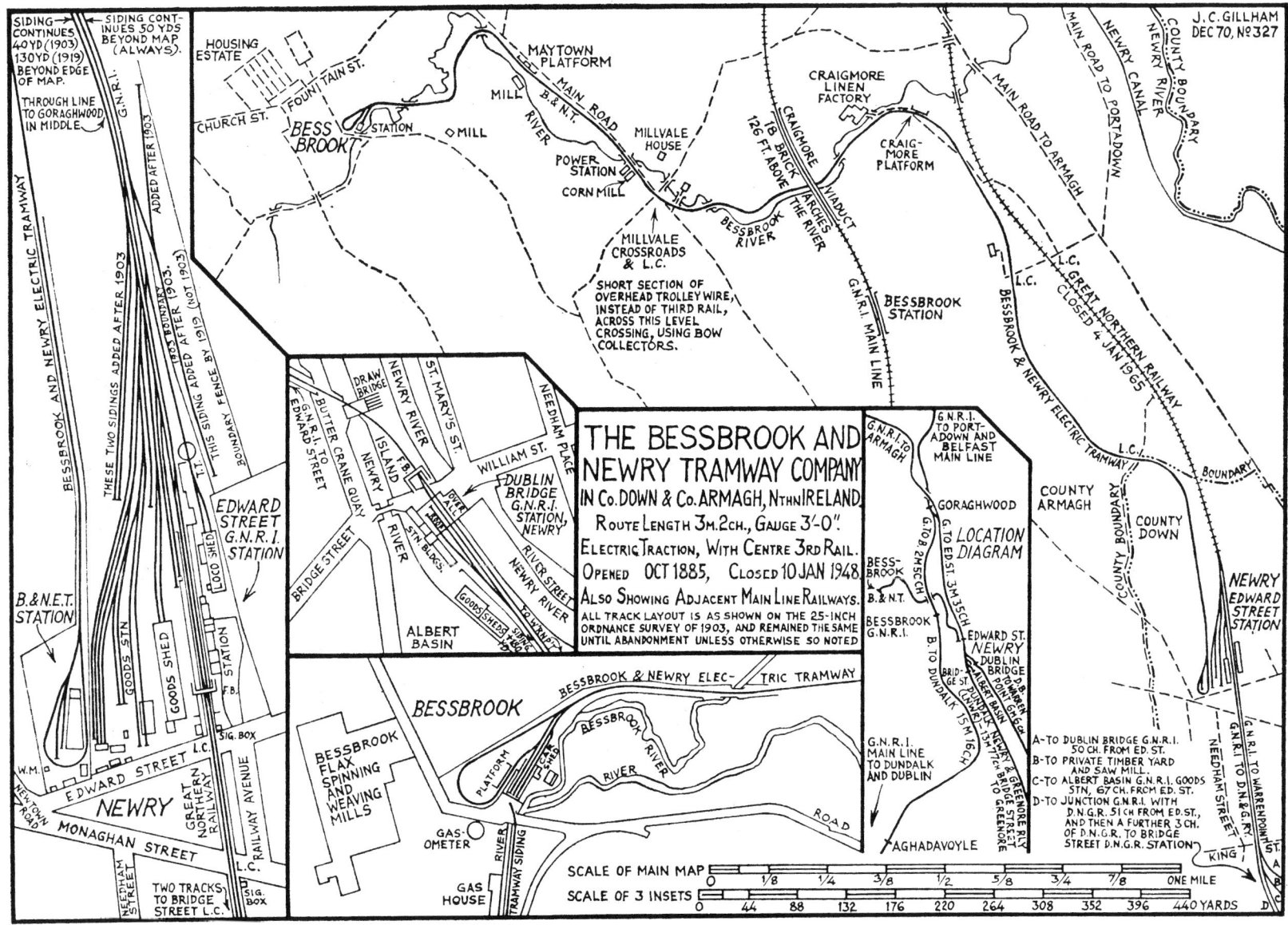

Newry Terminus looking south to the back of the buildings in Edward Street.

*W.J. Haynes*

Motor car No. 1 with flangeless open wagons at Millvale level crossing soon after opening.

*National Library of Ireland*

The first sod was cut on 8th September, 1883; however, it was considered advisable to seek official powers for the line, under the Tramways and Public Companies Act of that year (the 1881 Act had covered the original scheme); moreover, it had now been decided (on the advice of Dr Edward Hopkinson, an early electric pioneer) to work the line electrically, by harnessing the Camlough Stream at Millvale Road, where there was a 28 ft fall. Incidentally, the 1883 Act did not relate to electric traction, then in its infancy. The necessary powers were obtained on 26th May, 1884; meanwhile the work had been commenced, as regards earth cutting and embanking for the track formation. The General Engineer was J.L.D. Meares, of Newry, and the resident civil engineer F.S. Thomas of London. The *Newry Telegraph* expressed the hope that the new transport medium would not be confined to people in the 'Model Village' (Bessbrook) but that it would also be made available to the ordinary public.

Track-laying commenced at Edward Street, Newry, on 3rd November; meanwhile workmen were perfecting and completing bridges and cuttings. The contract for the electrical equipment had been given to Dr Edward Hopkinson, this equipment being supplied by Messrs Mather and Platt, the Manchester engineers, for the power station at Millvale. Meanwhile large slabs of granite, some weighing 5 tons, were on the site for laying in the millrace to support the turbine; the latter had already arrived from the makers Messrs McAdams of Belfast, also a base for the dynamos in the building beside the stream. (These premises had formerly been in the possession of A. W. Walker, JP). Later in the month, track laying had reached Craigmore, and the first instalment of the conductor rail had arrived; this was of channel iron (u-shaped cross section), and the contacts on the cars were to run on this.

Following the passing of the Order-in-Council, a company was formed, comprising John Grubb Richardson, James Nicholas Richardson, John F. Harris, and Henry Barcroft (Directors), also those who had subscribed to the undertaking, their executors and successors etc., the company being styled 'The Bessbrook and Newry Tramway', with a capital of £20,000 in £10 shares (of which only £15,000 were issued), also with powers to raise £6,500 in loans.

By July, 1885, laying of the conductor rail had been completed, and the first car, a bogie vehicle, was due to arrive at the Albert Basin, Newry, from Liverpool per the SS *Bessbrook*. However, on arrival, considerable difficulty was found in moving it to Monaghan Street for railing; this was subsequently overcome with the aid of a traction engine from the Spinning Mills. A month later, six open four-wheeled wagons arrived by sea, and were hauled to Newry terminus for railing. They could be used on rail or road (full details of both cars and wagons will appear later). Ramps were provided at each terminus (where there were also turning loops for cars) for unloading and re-railing the wagons.

The Board of Trade Inspection was made on 10th September, 1885 when at 12 noon a car and three wagons drew up at Edward Street terminus, where the car was boarded by General C.S. Hutchinson (Permanent Way and Rolling Stock Inspector), Major Armstrong (for the electrical gear), Messrs J.H. Harris, Henry Barcroft, J.L.D. Meares, CE (Engineer of the line), Henry Davison, (County Surveyor, Armagh), Dr John Hopkinson, FRS Dr Edward Hopkinson, electrical engineer (Messrs Mather and Platt), and Herbert Harrison, Manager and Secretary of the undertaking. The car then proceeded slowly towards Bessbrook, frequently stopping to allow General Hutchinson to examine underbridges and culverts. At Millvale, the live rail was replaced by an overhead power line, where the track crossed the road obliquely, the motor car roof being provided with a framework of bar iron (later replaced by an arm with bow collector), to make contact. From here the car continued to Bessbrook, passing the Halt at Maytown.

It was anticipated that the Inspector's Report would express satisfaction with the line, but this was not so. While satisfied with the solidly-built abutments and piers of bridges, some of which were all stone, and others having 23 ft wrought-iron spans, he condemned the lack of level crossing gates at Millvale, also at accommodation crossings.

The Company regarded these as unnecessary, but General Hutchinson considered them imperative for safety, also at private crossings, to prevent cattle straying on the line, and being injured or electrocuted by the live rail. Moreover, the gates must be so hung that they would tend to close across the track. Pending implementation of these requirements he would not sanction the line for public traffic. As regards the track, his Report showed that the 3 ft gauge line comprised flat-bottom steel rails 41.25 lbs per yard in 23 ft lengths; they were secured to the sleepers with dog spikes, except at sharp curves where bolts were also used, the timber sleepers being 6 ft x 5 in. x 4 in., laid at 3 ft intervals. Running rails were 3½ in. deep, and those on which the rail wagons ran were 25 lbs weight 2½ in. deep. The average gradient was 1 in 86, the steepest sections being 1 in 51, and 1 in 54, with a total fall from Bessbrook of 188 ft. (Note: Dr Hopkinson quotes the track weights as above, and the terminal loops 55 ft radius).

The electrical report from Major Armstrong was to follow, but there is no mention of its contents in local newspapers.

The company accordingly proceeded to carry out General Hutchinson's requirements regarding level crossing gates, and as regards those at Millvale, Mr Barcroft devised means to work them hydraulically, thus eliminating the need for a gateman (he was much interested in mechanical research). A cylinder, containing a float, and a cistern at a higher level, was erected near the power station. At points 50 yards from Millvale level crossing, posts with pivoted levers operating three-way cocks were installed. When a train reached one of these points an arm attached under the footboard of the leading car struck the lever, turning it fully over and causing the cock to empty the cylinder, and as the float therein

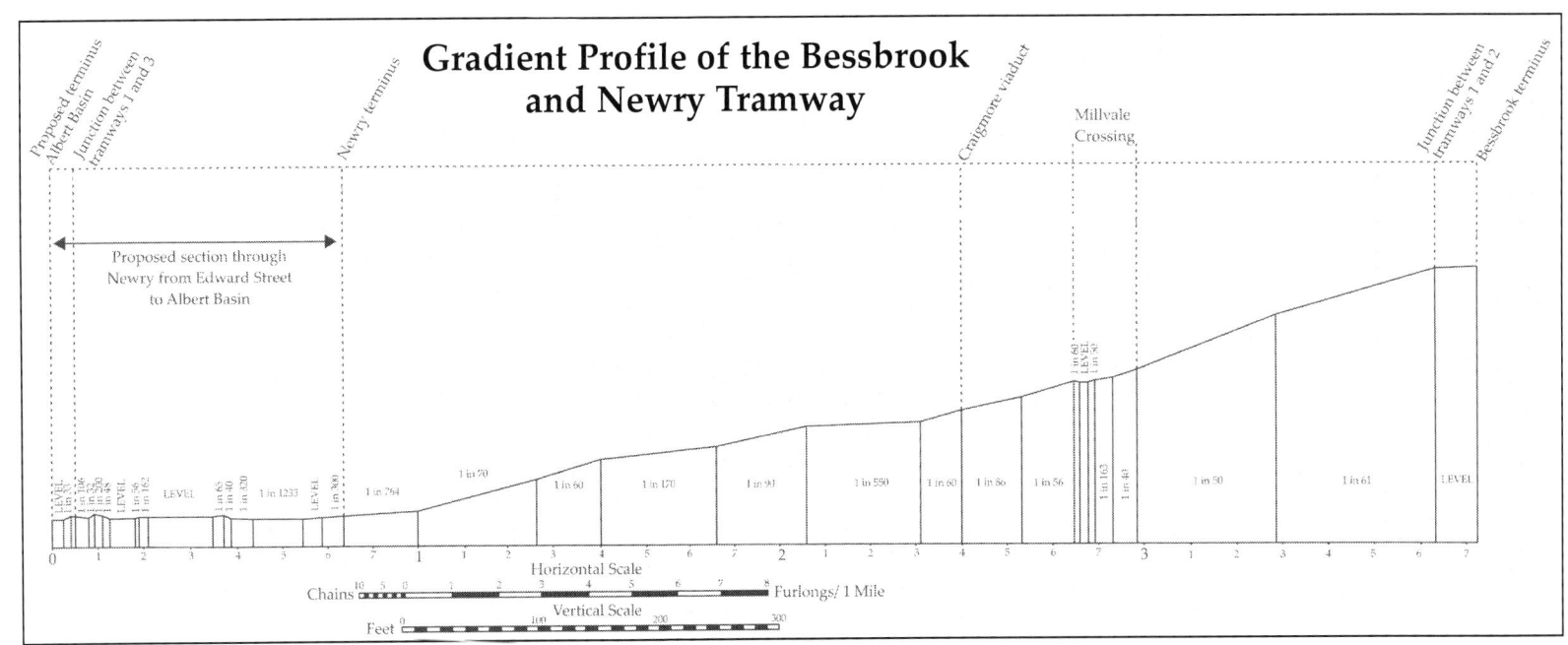

sank a wire rope attached to it opened the gates. On reaching the post on the far side a similar procedure but in reverse, followed, the cistern replenishing the cylinder, and as the float rose a second wire rope closed the gates. The Board of Trade had insisted that the gates must only open and close before and after a train passed. It was also laid down that the motor cars must be fitted with continuous brakes; otherwise a brakesman must ride on the last wagon. The cars, of course, had handbrakes.

Following implementation of the above, the Board of Trade Certificate was received on 3rd October; however, public traffic had commenced on 1st October, 1885, probably having been sanctioned by prior telegram. Numbers of country people availed themselves of the new facility to reach Newry Markets on the opening day, and within six weeks traffic had become so heavy that it was difficult to obtain accommodation on the last (10.30 pm) car on Saturday nights from Newry.

Neither the extension of line No. 1 to Albert Basin on Carlingford Road, nor line No. 3 to the Dundalk & Newry Steam Packet Company's warehouse at Albert Dock, was constructed. The plan with the provisional order (*see inside back cover*) shows some very tight curves, one of only three chains radius and two of 40 feet through Newry, but these may have been eased in construction.

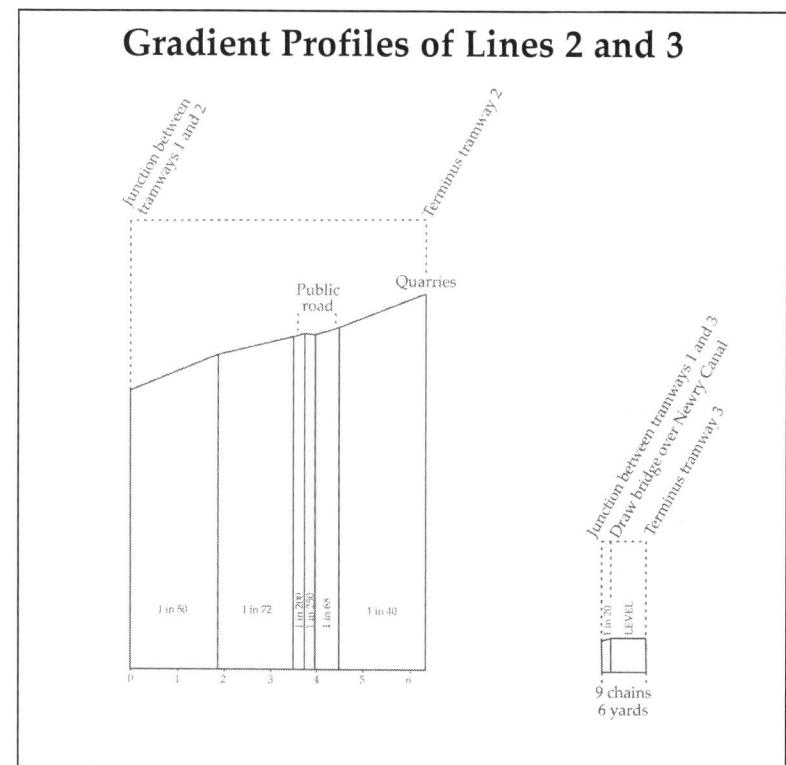

Car No. 6 at Bessbrook. The offset in height between the outer rails can be seen in this photograph.  *W.J. Haynes*

Inside Besscrook car shed, 12th May, 1937.

*C.J. Slator*

# Equipment

Details of the equipment were given by Dr Edward Hopkinson MA Dsc, to a meeting of the institute of Civil Engineers, recorded in its *Proceedings* No. 92 (pp 193-215), of 1887.

In July, 1884, Henry Barcroft, of the Spinning Mills, had suggested to Dr Hopkinson that the line be worked by electric traction, in view of the abundant water power. Negotiations with the Directors followed, resulting in a contract being given to Dr Hopkinson for the entire installation. Ten trains per day were to run each way, and the motored cars were to be capable of hauling 100 tons of goods each way, in addition to the tare of the cars and a full load of passengers; they were also to be able to haul 200 tons of minerals and goods per day. When hauling 18 tons in the Up direction the average speed was to be 6 mph, and in the case of 12 tons, a speed of 9 mph. The company undertook to place their line at the disposal of Dr Hopkinson for a period of time, and purchase the plant for a fixed sum, once the aforesaid conditions had been complied with, and a six months trial had proved that the working costs did not exceed those for steam traction on a similar line. The confidence of Dr Hopkinson and Henry Barcroft in the new traction medium was fully vindicated, and the company took over the line on 26th April, 1886.

## Turbines and Generators

The first-mentioned was an inward flow vortex wheel, with double buckets, working on a horizontal shaft, which extended into the dynamo premises, where the generators were driven direct by belting. The capacity of the turbine-wheel was 1,504 cubic feet per minute, the Camlough Stream having a flow of 3,000,000 gallons per day. When running at 290 revolutions per minute, the turbine would develop a maximum power of 62 HP, being worked with a tail draught of 13 ft. Admission of water was controlled by a shutter valve, regulating the flow uniformly through each bucket on the wheel and actuated either by hand or a centrifugal governor. The latter was not direct acting, but as its balls rose and fell beyond certain limits, they coupled one of a pair of right and left-hand bevel wheels driven by a wheel on the governor spindle to a small countershaft, geared with the valve spindle.

There were two generating dynamos of the Edison-Hopkinson type, manufactured by Messrs. Mather and Platt, Manchester. Each was shunt-wound, and intended for a normal output of 250 volts, 72 amps, at a speed of 1,000 revolutions per minute; but they were never used coupled, as one dynamo was found to be sufficient for the working of the line. Although the average current for a day's work did not exceed 72 amps, the current required for starting a heavy train on a steep gradient might be three times this amount. It was therefore essential that a dynamo intended for such purposes should not only be mechanically strong enough to develop an output far exceeding its normal output, but also that its design should be such that the variation in the lead of the brushes with the current should be as small as possible, and that the fall in electromotive force as the current increased should not be excessive. The latter conditions can be met by compound winding, but on the other hand the ease with which shunt machines could be coupled parallel was in favour of their use. It was also of considerable importance to keep the self-induction of the main circuit as a whole as low as possible, otherwise the sudden variations in current at starting and stopping trains was a severe strain on the insulation both of the generator and motor dynamos, and on the conductor cables. The resistance of the field magnet was 74 ohms and of the armature 0.12 ohm; consequently the electrical efficiency, when working with the normal current was 92.2 per cent and the commercial efficiency 90.4 per cent.

View along the track to the Craigmore viaduct, showing the conductor rail midway between the rails.  H. Fayle

## Conductor Rail

This was of channel steel, laid midway between the rails and carried on wooden insulators nailed to alternate sleepers. This form of rail does not require to be secured, but could be simply laid on the insulators which fit into the channel, and while allowing for longitudinal action to compensate for temperature changes, held it laterally. The joint had to be sufficiently strong mechanically and at the same time offer no electrical resistance. The electrical connection was therefore made independently of fish-plating by a strip of soft copper of such section that its conductivity was about the same as the steel. It was bent in the form of a 'U' to allow for expansion and contraction of the channel. These strips were riveted in the channel with double copper rivets, care having been taken that the hole in the channel was perfectly free of rust before riveting. At the several occupation crossings, 12 in number, the electrical continuity of the conductor was broken by insulating a section of the channel, current being conveyed by a cable beneath the sleepers. The top of the channel being level with the rails, the intervening space could be paved or planked, so making a good road. As the width of these crossings did not exceed the length of the locomotive car, the collector on the front bogie of this made contact with the conductor rail at the far side of the crossing before the collector on the rear bogie broke with the conductor rail.

## Overhead Equipment at Millvale Crossing

As this crossing was 150 ft in length, the method before described of bridging the gap was not feasible here. A copper wire was accordingly slung centrally between the rails from cross bars carried on posts, placed on each side of the rails at either end of the crossing, the lowest part of the catenary being 15 ft above road-level, to meet the requirements of the Board of Trade. An overhead collector, formed of bar iron, fixed above the roof of the car, passed under the crossbar and immediately made contact with the wire before the back collector left the ground conductor (i.e. live rail), and continued to make a rubbing contact with the wire until the leading collector had again made contact with the ground conductor on the other side of the crossing. This method of carrying the conductor and making contact with it was designed in 1885 by Dr Hopkinson's brother, Dr John Hopkinson, FRS, and proved in every way a complete success. The car roof collector, though merely a bar of flat-iron one inch wide greased with tallow once a week, made a perfect contact with the copper wire sufficiently good for transmitting 120 amps. After two years experience there was no perceptible wear on the wire except at the point where it was picked up by the collector, and even here it was very small. An overhead conductor has many advantages over one at ground level or beneath; there is no interference with crossings, it is less subject to malicious or accidental injury, and particularly, perfect insulation

The only road crossing on the line, 2 miles from Newry, showing the short length of catenary needed to supply current.  *H. Fayle*

and isolation can be secured, enabling currents of much higher potential to be used with safety. Some animals cannot stand a shock of 300 volts, and it was likely the Board of Trade would not sanction the use of any higher potential if there was a possibility of the conductor being accidentally touched. Nevertheless, the difficulty of making contact with an overhead conductor had hitherto opposed almost insuperable difficulties, now obviated by the above simple device. Two catenaries were used, with the points of support at different levels, in order to reduce the tension of the wire, and the pull on the posts, which in this instance were not balanced by a like pull on the opposite side, as would have been the case were the conductor constructed throughout on that principle. The wires were of hand-drawn copper, No. 4 BWG (Birmingham Wire Guage, 0.238 in./6.045 mm), and the actual tension was 120 lbs. The collector cleared the underside of the crossbar by 5½ in., and therefore picked up the conductor 64 in. from the posts.

The insulators upon which the channel steel (ground) conductor were supported were blocks of poplar wood 5 in. long, carefully dried and then impregnated with boiling paraffin. A block of dried poplar would absorb as much as 75 per cent of its own weight of paraffin, which permeated through the whole mass. These blocks proved to be efficient insulators, and were apparently standing well. The circuit was completed by the rails of the permanent way, which were uninsulated. As in the case of the conductor the fishplate connections were not sufficient, and were supplemented with flexible copper strips riveted to the under sides of the rails, which were of Barrow Hematite steel.

The rails were practically insulated by the sleepers and dry ballast. A curious confirmation of this occurred during a severe thunderstorm. At the first flash a man employed at the Newry end of the line, who was touching the running rail when standing on wet ground, received a smart shock. Simultaneously the power station attendant observed a blaze of light from the earth brush of the generating dynamo. At the second flash a similar discharge was observed, and at a third more intense flash, the same occurred again, and the fusible plug connecting the conductor with the dynamos gave way. Two men at the Bessbrook end of the line touching the running rails, but not the conductor, received severe shocks. Clearly in each case the system as a whole had been struck, and the charge was making the best of its way to earth. After this occurrence, the running rails were provided with earth connections at several points.

## Passenger Cars

The locomotive equipment consisted of two passenger cars (Nos., 1 and 2) 33 ft and 21 ft 8 in. long respectively, each provided with a motor. The car bodies were carried on two four-wheel bogies, with a wheelbase of 4 ft 6 in., the motor being carried on the front bogie independent of the car body; this enabled the cars to negotiate the curves at the termini with great facility, and also relieved the body of the car from vibration due to the driving. The body of the larger car was divided into three compartments; the front one covered the motor, the second formed a second-class compartment seating 24

Rear end of car No. 2 on 16th August 1938.    E.W. Hannan

The front of car No. 2 with No. 6 as trailer, showing the arrangement of the bogies.

*H. Fayle*

Car No. 4 with van No. 2 and brake van No. 6 at Millvale level crossing on 17th April 1940.

*W.A. Camwell*

passengers, and, was separated by a cross passage from the first-class section, seating 10. The bogie, carrying the motor, had an extended platform, projecting 3 ft 7 in. beyond the car body, communicating by a sliding door with the dynamo compartment, thus affording the driver access to all parts of the driving machinery, which was, in turn, partitioned off from the passenger accommodation. All four wheels were braked by a powerful screw brake, worked from the front (dash) of the driving platform, on which was also fitted the switchboard controlling the motor. The wheels of the rear car were braked by a chain brake, operated from the cross passage by the conductor. This brake was also arranged for coupling to the wagons. The total weight of the cars was 8¼ tons distributed as follows:-

| | | |
|---|---|---|
| Car body | 3 t | 6 cwt 1 qr* |
| Leading bogie | 1 t | 17 cwt 2 qr |
| Trailing | 1 t | 0 cwt 0 qr |
| Dynamo, bedplate, and accessories | 2 t | 1 cwt 1 qr |
| TOTAL | 8 t | 5 cwt 0 qr |

* There are 20 hundredweight (cwt) in a ton, and 4 quarters (qr) in a hundredweight.

The shorter car was similar, but without the 1st class compartment. Both cars were built by the Ashbury Carriage Co., Manchester. There was also a 3rd car (No. 3), a trailer, of the same length as No. 1, seating 44 passengers, and carried on two four-wheel bogies. This car weighed 5½ tons, and was constructed by the Starbuck Company, Birkenhead. It is not known how long first class was retained.

## Car Motors

Each locomotive-car was fitted with an Edison-Hopkinson dynamometer. As previously mentioned, the motor was fixed on the leading bogie, and was entirely independent of the body of the car. The armature shaft carried a double helical toothed steel pinion 6.05 in. in diameter, gearing into a steel wheel 21.08 in. in diameter, carried on a small countershaft running in bearings fixed on the bed of the motor. This shaft also carried a chain pinion wheel of steel 8.8 in. diameter, on the extended boss of which the helical toothed wheel was keyed. The chain pinion drove with chain gear on to a wheel 21 in. in diameter, keyed on to the back axle of the bogie, the wheels of which were 28 in. in diameter. This gave a ratio of gear 8.3 to 1; hence a speed of 1 mile per hour corresponded to 100 revolutions per minute of the dynamo axle. To give the necessary adhesion, the axles were coupled with outside connecting rods.

The motors were series-wound, with such a number of convolutions that the magnets were nearly saturated with 72 amps, which was also the normal current for the armature. The resistance of the magnets was 0.113 ohms and of the armature 0.112 ohm; hence, if the potential between the terminals was 220 volts, the electrical efficiency with the normal current was 92.6 per cent, and the commercial efficiency 90.7 per cent, the power developed being

Car No. 1 with trailer No. 3.                    A.T. Newham collection

nearly 20 HP. In actual work the power of the motor frequently exceeded this amount. To transmit this power with the car running at for example, 7 mph, the tension of the chain would have been 1,430 lbs and the speed 400 ft per minute. At starting on a gradient with a full load, the tension could reach 3,400 lbs, and with the car running at the maximum rate, the speed might reach 1,300 ft per minute. Considerable difficulty was experienced in obtaining a chain strong enough to stand the high working tension, and at the same time not unduly heavy for running at the high speed. Several chains of the well-known tricycle form were tried (but defects developed). A steel chain, specially constructed by Mr Hans Renold was finally tried, in which the tubes were keyed as well as riveted in the inner links, and the pins in the outer, and the (former) rollers abandoned. The average breaking strain of the steel was 43½ tons per square inch.

## Wagons

These were of particular interest in that they were flange-less, to permit of use on public roads as well as rail. The wheels were loose on the axles and the latter free to rotate on their journals. On the tramway, an ingenious arrangement had been devised by Mr Henry Barcroft, comprising a set of rails laid at a lower level outside the (car) running rails, the latter serving as flanges to keep the wagons in place. This idea was originally suggested, in 1880, by Mr Alfred E. Holt, M.Inst.C.E., and embodied in the Lancashire Plateways scheme, for which a Bill was lodged in the Autumn of 1882, and subsequently withdrawn. The device was later worked out in practical detail by Mr Barcroft of Newry. The tyres of the wheels were 2¾ in wide, which was sufficient for use on ordinary roads. The buffers were fixed on the truck frame, no buffing being done against the fore-carriage. A single central coupling engaged in a jaw on the latter. The weight of each wagon, without the shafts for road haulage was 23¼ cwt, and the wagons were of sufficient strength to carry two ton loads. This was not excessive for a single horse to haul, where there were no steep gradients; on the latter, two horses were necessary. Twenty-two of these wagons were supplied (by 1887) by the Ashbury Carriage Company, Manchester.

The cars and wagons were painted mahogany brown, with the title 'Bessbrook and Newry Tramway' on the side panels below the windows in small block letters, the serial numbers, prefixed 'No.' appearing in the centre of the lower panels of the cars. Later, the numbers were moved up to the end of the titles on the car sides, the wagons being similarly lettered on their side planks. In later days, one car at least had the initials 'B. and N.T. No. 2' in large block capitals on the side panels below the windows.

## Description of Line

The line commenced at the Edward Street station of the Newry branch of the Great Northern Railway (Ireland) (GNR(I)), and ran parallel to it for about ¾ mile; then passing through a cutting, it followed the course of the Camlough Stream. Not far from the Craigmore viaduct it reached the first station near Craigmore village and an outlying mill of the Bessbrook Spinning Co. Proceeding up the valley on a 1 in 50 gradient it crossed the county road diagonally by a level crossing near which was the second station, Millvale. Here it crossed the Camlough Stream ¾ mile from Millvale and then ran to the terminus at Bessbrook, where there was a station and carriage shed. Further intermediate halts were provided at Mullaglass and Maytown.

The gauge was 3 ft and the line single track, but land had been acquired for a double line. At each terminus there was a turning loop, so that cars did not need reversing, except when coupling up wagons or shunting in the sidings. The permanent way was laid out and constructed under the supervision of Mr J.L.D. Meares. (Platforms were provided at each terminus, also at intermediate stations, that at Newry apparently being at first parallel with

Open and closed flangeless wagons. Behind the wagons is the goods shed that sat in the loop of line at the Newry terminus.   *H. Fayle*

Bessbrook terminus, car No. 1 sits closest to the camera in front of the engine shed. To the right of the shed is the short platform. In the background Bessbrook Mill can be seen behind the trees. The line off to the right leads to the turning loop. *Oakwood collection*

Edward Street, but later beside the boundary wall of the Great Northern Railway station. Also, at Newry there were two sidings inside the loop, one providing a 'take-off-and-on' for wagons between rail and road and vice-versa; another was provided at Bessbrook, south of the turning loop. The wagon rails were not provided on the turning loops.)

## Cost of Construction

The cost of the electrical equipment may be briefly summarized as follows:-

| | | | |
|---|---|---|---|
| Turbine, pentrough, and driving gear | £300 | 0s. | 0d. |
| Two generator dynamos, measuring instruments and driving belts | £450 | 0s. | 0d. |
| Conductor (rail) @£200 per mile | £600 | 0s. | 0d. |
| Two locomotive cars, including entire electrical equipment | £1,120 | 0s. | 0d. |
| Total | £2,470 | 0s. | 0d. |

Each of the above items including delivery and erection.

## Cost of Working

The cost of haulage was carefully ascertained over a period of five months from 21st November, 1885, to 2nd April, 1886.

| | | | |
|---|---|---|---|
| Wages of driver and attendant at generator station | £32 | 7s. | 6d. |
| Sundry Repairs | £6 | 1s. | 0d. |
| Oil, grease, and waste | £5 | 4s. | 0d. |
| Rental of water power | £59 | 16s. | 0d. |
| Dynamo brushes, renewals of driving chain, and commutators | £14 | 11s. | 6d. |
| TOTAL | £118 | 0s. | 0d. |

Train mileage = 8,652. Cost per train mile = 3s. 3d.

For the six months ending 30th June, 1887, during which period there had been a goods traffic of 8,000 tons over the line, a much larger amount than in the period referred to above, the cost per train mile was somewhat greater, as follows:-

| | | | |
|---|---|---|---|
| Wages | £50 | 18s. | 0d. |
| Sundry repairs and alterations including cost of changing the winding of four armatures of the dynamos | £341 | 4s. | 3d. |
| Oil, grease and waste | £10 | 0s. | 0d. |
| Rental of water power | £71 | 15s. | 0d. |
| Dynamo brushes and sundry renewals | £12 | 5s. | 10d. |
| TOTAL | £486 | 3s. | 1d. |

Train mileage = 10,171. Cost per train mile = 4s. 2d.

Figures do not include depreciation or supervision.

Open trailer No. 5 as built.    *Hurst Nelson*

The second car No.1 which replaced the earlier one in 1911.

*H. Fayle*

Bogie trailer car No. 3.

*H. Fayle*

Motor car No. 4.

H. Fayle

## Operation (and Mishaps)

Within a week of the line's opening, an anonymous letter, signed 'A Lady' appeared in the *Newry Telegraph* stating 'this mere notice of the objectionable practice of smoking, chewing tobacco, and spitting in the cars will, it is hoped, cause the nuisance to be prohibited. If smoking is a necessity, then let the 1st class compartment be allocated for this'. No action would appear to have been taken at the time, as on 12th November a further complaint appeared from the same source alleging that the atmosphere in a car of the 10.30 pm service from Newry was offensive and oppressive, clouds of smoke obscuring other passengers; if allowed to continue, 'respectable' people would be obliged to find other means of 'going that way'.

On 6th February, 1886, a slight mishap occurred, when the Up car was approaching Newry, a chain broke, and passengers were obliged to walk to the platform. Here other passengers were waiting to board the car for its return journey at 12.15 pm, the result being that they had to wait until the next car arrived from Bessbrook.

On 9th April, a number of minor mishaps occurred, a wagon was derailed, the wheel of a passenger car broke, whilst a chain sent as a replacement broke away. However, only minor inconvenience resulted, and the passenger services were satisfactorily maintained.

In February 1887, it was announced that a petition would be submitted to the Privy Council for leave to abandon spurs from each terminal, originally authorized by the Order-in-Council of 1883 (see earlier). The application duly came before the Privy Council on the 24th February and presumably was granted. Nevertheless, spur 1 appears to have been built at some future date as it was still extant in 1965. It crossed a public road, continuing on private right-of-way, the nearer end being paved with square granite setts.

On 19th May, the *Irish Builder* contained an article on the line wherein it was stated that the cars were capable of 15 mph, but to conform with established rules only did 8 to 10 mph. Since opening, 30,000 miles had been run, 150,000 passengers carried, and 15,000 tons of goods transported. The cost of working a full car, including cost of wages, repairs, and rental of water power was 4$d$. per mile.

On 7th June, an accident occurred at 3 pm. The car involved was only about 100 yards on its journey to Bessbrook, with two heavily laden wagons of coal, when a wagon axle broke, upsetting the vehicle; an employee of the company, Diffin, was sitting on top of the load, and was thrown heavily to the ground. The car at once stopped, when it was found that the man fortunately had only a few slight bruises. (The B.o.T. Inspector had stipulated that, as no guard's vans were being provided, a man must sit on the last wagon.)

In 1888, some interesting facts were furnished respecting housing at Bessbrook. As families preferred to reside in houses rather than the flat blocks, weekly rents ranged from 1$s$. to 4$s$. per week; a house having a parlour, kitchen and scullery, with two bedrooms upstairs, cost 2$s$. 6$d$. weekly. Outside the village was a large tract of land, divided up into plots, which were let for a small sum, enabling the inhabitants to grow sufficient vegetables to last them for most of the year. There was also a medical and education fund, each costing 1$d$. a week, no other fees being charged. The mill workers were paid 8$s$. to 9$s$. a week, some receiving more, and managers received £500 per year. The village Institute (the gift of Mrs Richardson) had a library with over 1,000 volumes. John Grubb Richardson was landlord of the entire village, which had a population of 4,000, and was run on model lines.

In February 1890, a power failure, fortunately of short duration occurred, a car en route to Bessbrook coming to a halt at a point unattractively named 'Pig Hall Loaning'. Four years later, another derailment occurred, two wagons leaving the track outside Stewart McKnight's 'pub' at Millvale crossing, but after a short delay, they were re-railed. (The scanty amount of information concerning the tramway during these years is regrettable, but is due to the relevant Minute Books having proved untraceable.)

On 22nd February, 1898, fire broke out about 2 am at Bessbrook Spinning Mills. The night watchman discovered smoke emanating from the preparing room and at once raised the alarm, and the Mill horn was sounded. The works Fire Brigade being on the spot very shortly. Aided by volunteers, two jets of water were soon attacking the flames and after an hour's hard work, the blaze was under control, another hour extinguishing it. The local constabulary also gave valuable assistance. Unfortunately much of the machinery, then new, also an engine adjoining the factory, was destroyed, and this was expected to result in many of the workers being idle for quite a time.

A few months later on 14th May, a horse was electrocuted on the tramway; Mrs McKnight and a friend were driving home from Newry when, crossing the tramway the horse suddenly fell. Both ladies were thrown heavily to the ground, and the young man driving ran to the assistance of the horse, only to find it was dead.

On 27th December, a large representative body of local traders and residents, with Thomas Macken in the chair, met in the Market Hall, Newtownhamilton, to consider a proposed new narrow gauge railway, the Newry, Keady and Tynan Light Railway (NKT), which would serve Newtownhamilton, amongst other towns. All present declared themselves in favour of the scheme, expressing willingness to promote it in every way possible. Brief speeches stressing its great advantages followed, suitable Resolutions being passed (there were no other railways in the area).

Eleven months later (25th November, 1899) the official application for powers appeared in the *Dublin Gazette*. Whether by coincidence or not, a notice also appeared alongside it from the Great Northern Railway (Ireland) seeking powers for a branch from Armagh to Keady.

As regards the NKT line, the promoters proposed seeking agreements with the GNR(I) and the Dundalk, Newry and Greenore Railway (DNG), a third rail to be laid on all sidings of the first-mentioned undertaking's goods yard at Newry and a connecting spur from the Bessbrook and Newry Tramway; also the provision of a third rail on the DNG. (in connection with the latter, R. A. Macroy, Chairman of the Dundalk, Newry and Greenore put in a letter favouring the scheme, and recommending it to the London & North Western Railway's Board, as it would make a through route for traffic via Greenore to the English markets, as there was no port at Newry). From Bessbrook the NKT line would join that of the Bessbrook and Newry, continuing via Darkley, Newtownhamilton, Keady, Norton's Cross, Middletown and Tynan to Caledon. Running powers would be sought over the Clogher Valley Railway, with a connecting link, while the Bessbrook and Newry Tramway would be leased or purchased, thus completing the scheme. (This, of course, would have meant converting the latter from electric to steam working.)

The Bill came before the British Parliament at the 1900 Spring Session, and was passed; however, no construction of the lines followed. It may be that difficulty arose about raising the capital.

In February 1900 Newry Council met to consider the Bill for the Newry, Keady and Tynan Light Railway whereby they would be authorized to guarantee the 4 per cent dividend on £50,000 of that company's share Capital. (This suggests that the railway was to be built under the powers of the 1883 Tramways [Ireland] Act.)

On 4th June, the Bessbrook and Newry Tramway directors met, Barcroft now being Chairman, and a letter from a Miss Newton was considered, seeking a reduction of fares if a number of tickets were bought at one time. It was decided to make a 25 per cent reduction, provided 50 tickets were bought at the same time. Agreement had also been reached with the promoters of the Newry, Keady & Tynan Light Railway, and the matter was now with the company's solicitors.

Mr J.L.D. Meares, who had been supervising engineer of the line when it was built, offered to inspect it for a fee of £6 6s.; Barcroft was therefore asked to see him, and endeavour to secure a reduction of a guinea, but failing this, to settle for the amount. It transpired that the inspection was to be a very full one, so the point was not pressed. Meares submitted his report on 7th July, 1900, and this showed the following requirements:- 1,100 to 1,200 new

Car No. 1 at Newry terminus, over the wall backing the platform is the goods yard of the Great Northern Railway.

*Oakwood collection*

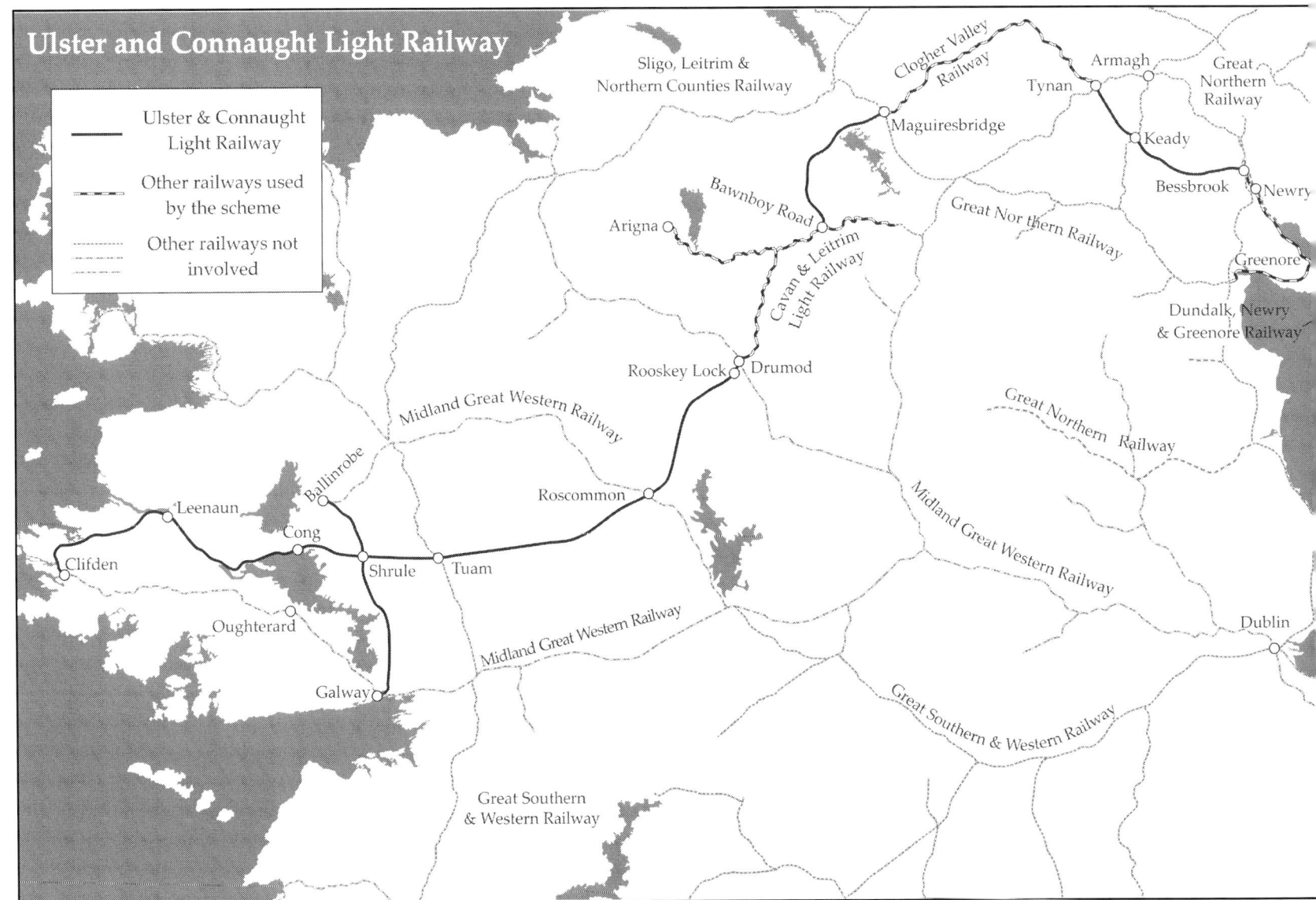

sleepers, re-packing of rails and sleepers in many places; water tables and outer drains to be cleaned, the latter to provide an outfall, and the first-mentioned to keep the ballast dry; track weeding; re-timbering points and crossings; renewing Millvale crossing; more ballast required, also extra fencing posts.

On 23rd July, a discussion was held concerning loss of power, due to the conductor rail being worn. There was a half-year's profit of £218 12s. 3d., compared with £162 16s. 7d., the increase comprising a special credit of £82 17s. 7d. paid by the owners of the SS *Bessbrook* for hauling coals. At this time either the manager, or the Newry station master (it is not clear which) had a most onerous job; he was to see the first car depart at 8.30 am on weekdays (10 am Sundays) and the last car at 10.30 pm; also to travel on the latter occasionally, to ensure the bye-laws were not infringed. In alternate weeks, he was to attend the departure of the 5.30 am workers' car, yet still be on duty at 10.30 pm! He also had to see that the office clerk at Newry was neat, clean, and did not mess the books with ink. He was also to make spot checks at odd times. on the worker's car in 'late turn' weeks.

The manager was instructed to order four top coats for the car crews, also waterproof suits for permanent way men (in those days the cars only had low dashes, and no windscreens). It was resolved that Christmas Day would be a staff holiday and that passengers were no longer to be permitted to travel in the covered brake van – the first mention of this vehicle.

In June, 1901, it was stated that McClure (former station master at Newry) was to return to his former post there. His predecessor, M'Partland, had lost an empty case consigned for dispatch, and as a result of a claim for 10s., this was to be recouped from him in two instalments; this, however, was not a reason for his dismissal. M'Clure was also paid 2s. extra to sit up at night, in lieu of coal money, and weigh incoming loads of coal; one wonders when his employers expected him to sleep! By mid-April, the conductor rail had become worn, so 100 new lengths were installed, and it was resolved to keep a supply in stock for future renewals.

Early in 1902, the 12.30 pm tram from Newry was involved in a mishap, owing to a derailed wagon, which struck and felled two of the posts carrying the overhead, and breaking the connections. It was found that the posts were rotten, and replacements were erected, with the assistance of staff from Bessbrook, who also assisted in clearing the road, and the connections were re-made, but services were suspended until 5.30 am the following morning. As the other two posts were found to be rotten, instructions were issued to replace them also. The accident proved to be due to a sunken running rail.

In August, the following correct list of rolling stock was furnished:- 2 electromotive cars, 1 passenger car (trailer); one covered passenger van; 19 peat wagons, Nos. 1 to 16 (excluding No. 4); also Nos. 21, 22, 26, 27 and six covered ditto, Nos. 17, 18, 20, 23, 24, 25 (presumably wagon No. 19 had been scrapped).

Three months later, the Newry, Keady & Tynan Light Railway scheme was revived, under the revised title of Ulster and Connaught Light Railway, with expanded plans. They sought:

1. to obtain extended time to purchase the Bessbrook and Newry Tramway;
2. to secure increased capital and borrowing powers;
3. power to work the Clogher Valley, also Cavan and Leitrim, Railways;
4. to acquire the Arigna Mining Co. Ltd.;
5. to reach agreements with the Shannon Navigation Co. in respect of their steamer services, and other railways ( they also intended laying a 3rd rail to the Dundalk, Newry and Greenore Railway at Newry).

The Bill was to be promoted in the 1903 Spring Session of the British Parliament. Although Leitrim County Council were initially in favour of the project, by May 1903 they thoroughly disapproved of the project. The Cavan and Leitrim Railway directors succeeded in dissuading them, being desirous of building their own branch to the mines at Gubbarudda from Arigna, as well as an extension of their main line to Rooskey Lock, from Drumod, both extensions the Ulster and Connaught planned to build.

However, by the time the Ulster and Connaught scheme reached its second reading, its aspirations had been much curtailed, although it still retained the plan to build an extension from the western terminus of the Clogher Valley Railway at Maguiresbridge (where the latter met the Dundalk-Enniskillen branch of the GNR(I)), and running southwards to meet the Cavan and Leitrim Railway by a reverse loop at Bawnboy Road station also the Arigna mines branch. Meanwhile, the GNR(I). had strongly objected to the project as regards its Newry end, in that it would abstract traffic which the railway company had built up by its own enterprise. The Bill eventually got through Parliament as an unopposed measure, but again no construction ensued. Previously (April) the promoters had circulated a map showing future extensions: Newry to Rostrevor, and via the coast on to Newcastle, Co. Down; also from Newry via Rathfriland to Ballyroney. It should be added that the Bessbrook and Newry Tramway, and the Bessbrook Spinning Company had also previously petitioned against the Ulster and Connaught Light Railway's scheme. Nevertheless in 1903 it was proposed to extend the line from Rooskey Lock, via Strokestown (Co. Roscommon) to Shrule, Co. Galway, whence branches would diverge north to Ballinrobe, and south to Galway, the main line continuing through North Connemara, via Cong and Leenaun, finally turning south to Clifden. The chances of this section paying were remote, as apart from some tourist traffic in summer, there would be few passengers, and little goods traffic owing to the sparse population; moreover, the Midland Great Western Railway already had a line from Galway (and Dublin) to Clifden, via central Connemara, which can hardly have paid in winter, due to similar conditions beyond Oughterard. However, no powers were sought for the above extension which, if built, would have constituted a mileage of 238 of narrow-gauge track across Ireland – longer than the standard-gauge Great Southern and Western Railway line from Dublin to Valentia Harbour, Co. Kerry. Needless to relate, nothing more was heard of such an uneconomic scheme. Two years later (23rd March, 1905) a press report announced that a prospectus for the Newry, Keady & Tynan Light Railway (the original project) would appear at the end of the month. In May, application was made to Parliament for the suspension of Standing Orders, to enable a clause to be included in the earlier Act, revising the title as above.

Following the usual legal complications, the revised Bill passed its second reading in the House of Lords, but as stated previously, no construction took place, notwithstanding a further application for powers four years later; even as late as 1912 there were still references to it in newspapers. Meantime, the Bessbrook & Newry Tramway continued its somewhat leisurely progress, seemingly without untoward incident; the Minute Books for this period are unfortunately not available.

In November, 1905, Henry Barcroft, DL, who had had so much to do with the tramway, was seriously ill at his Dublin residence at Baldoyle, whither he had moved from Newry some years previously, on account of failing health. He passed away on the 18th November. In addition to having been Managing Director of the Bessbrook Spinning Mills, also a Director of the Dundalk and Newry Steam Packet Co., he had taken a prominent part in public affairs in Newry. For 15 years High Sheriff of County Armagh, he was subsequently Deputy Lieutenant of the county. He was also associated with Newry Technical Institute, and in view of taking a keen interest in mechanical research was elected a member of the Institute of Civil Engineers.

The Minute Books for 1912/13 contain little of import. In December 1912, it was announced that a shelter would be erected at Newry terminus for the benefit of mill workers arriving for the 5.30 am car. Early in 1913, orders were given that four large wheels and two small ones, also eight axles, were to be painted and the car bodies varnished. The reference to large wheels is mystifying, as the cars did not then have maximum traction trucks, otherwise reference would have been made to four large wheels and four small ditto, and a similar number of axles. On 3rd April, when the 10.25 pm tram was on its journey, two wagons were derailed, and an axle of the brake van broken. Nine months later (14th January, 1914)

Newry terminus looking north with car No. 4 waiting at the platform, August 1938.

*E.W. Hannan*

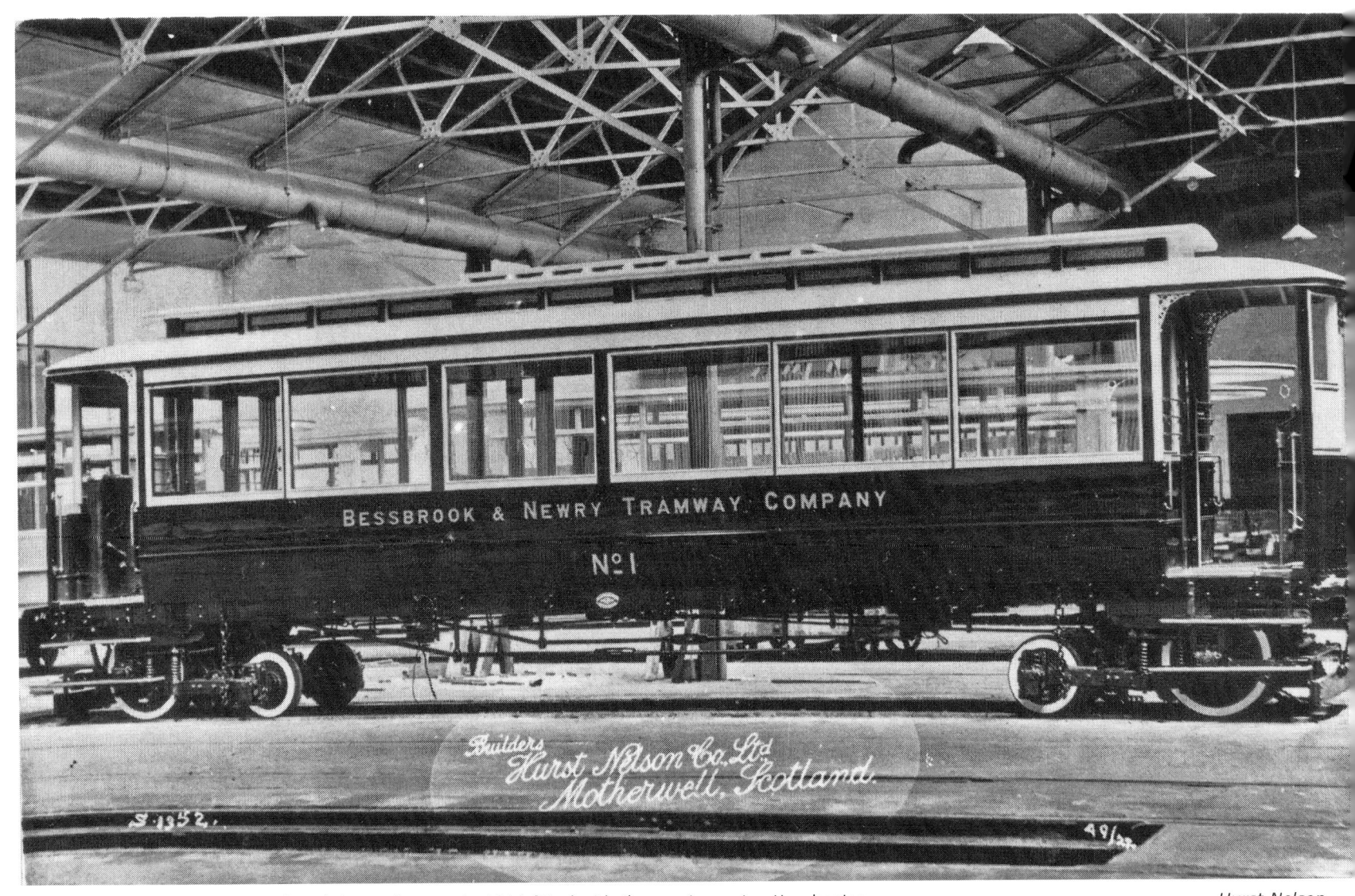

New No. 1 car which replaced the earlier one in 1911 fitted with the maximum traction bogies.

*Hurst Nelson*

another derailment occurred, this time respecting an empty wagon attached to the 11.20 am Down tram, which left the track at Craigmore viaduct; the Minutes record laconically that the staff concerned would therefore lose their bonus. Presumably this payment referred to accident-free operation of the service. Such incidents suggest that either the outer edges of the tramcar running rails had become worn, or that the inner faces of the wagon wheels had worn down, thus making them loose to gauge.

On 25th January, 1915, instructions were issued that the 'driving car' was to be shedded on Fridays and thoroughly cleaned, with inspection of the covers (presumably the seats) by Foreman Watson. Six months later it was announced that a special car was to run from Bessbrook to Newry for about two months, calling at Craigmore on Monday, Tuesday, Thursday and Friday nights.

By February 1918 fuel supplies at the Spinning Mills had apparently run low, as orders were given that the 5.30 am worker's car ex-Newry, on arrival at Bessbrook, was to return at once to Newry, to bring up coal supplies; in addition, there were to be a few all-night workings, if possible, until a good stock had been built up at the Mills.

On 10th June, by Order of the Irish Railway Executive, all fares were to be increased by 50 per cent from 1st July (similar increases were ordered on various railways, also the Dublin and Lucan Electric Railway). On 25th November the following service was announced:- 6.10 am ex-Bessbrook, Mondays to Fridays. Ex-Newry, 7.20 am, Monday to Friday, 3 pm, 4 pm, 5 pm, 7.30 pm, 8.00 pm, 9.30 pm. Three weeks later, notice was given that no service would operate on Christmas and St Stephens (Boxing) Days, but a late 'extra' would leave Newry at 10.30 pm (we are not informed if this related to Christmas Eve, or St Stephens Day!). Meanwhile a large wagon, measuring 16 ft by 12 ft was to be ordered from Messrs Ross and Ross, Newry. Shortly after the beginning of 1919, the Irish Railway Executive informed the company that a 48-hour week was to be allotted to their staff, under one of the following bases: (a) a system of split working turns of duty, already drawn up, requiring the employment of an extra man, and an office boy; or (b) an alternative plan if the staff turned down the above, involving employment of four extra employees was to be introduced; hardly surprisingly, the staff rejected the first scheme, and on 3rd February, the Manager reported having taken on the extra men (the British Government, earlier in the year, had passed an Act enforcing an eight-hour day, 48 hours per week for all railwaymen). By the end of March, the wage-earning staff comprised a total of seven men.

On 14th April, it was announced that no services would operate on 21st and 22nd April, these dates coinciding with the Easter holiday; incidentally, there was never any service on 12th July (the Northern Ireland National holiday).

At the beginning of February 1920, the B&N Tramway Manager, with the consultant engineer (McDowell) had a meeting with Ingram, Secretary of the Ministry of Transport in Dublin respecting rates (of pay?) and the need to repair the passenger rolling stock and replace the now out-of-date Power Plant. It was agreed that the cost of the latter would be borne entirely by the British Government, but renewal of cars would be the responsibility of the company, at 1913 costs, the excess above this to be borne by the Government.

Colonel O'Brien, Electrical Engineer to the Ministry of Transport, visited Bessbrook on 22nd March, and inspected the cars and the generating plant, announcing that his Report would follow subsequently. This arrived by 3rd May. In it, Colonel O'Brien advocated the replacement of Car No. 1, but considered that the power plant would last for another two to three years. This was considered most unsatisfactory, and it was resolved to have a suitable reply sent to the Ministry of Transport. Meanwhile it was also decided to order a new car from Messrs Hurst Nelson, of Motherwell, and to renew the bodywork of No. 2 car. Also to order a new turbine and generating plant from Messrs G. Gilkes, of Kendal, England, as the British Government had previously undertaken to bear the cost of the latter.

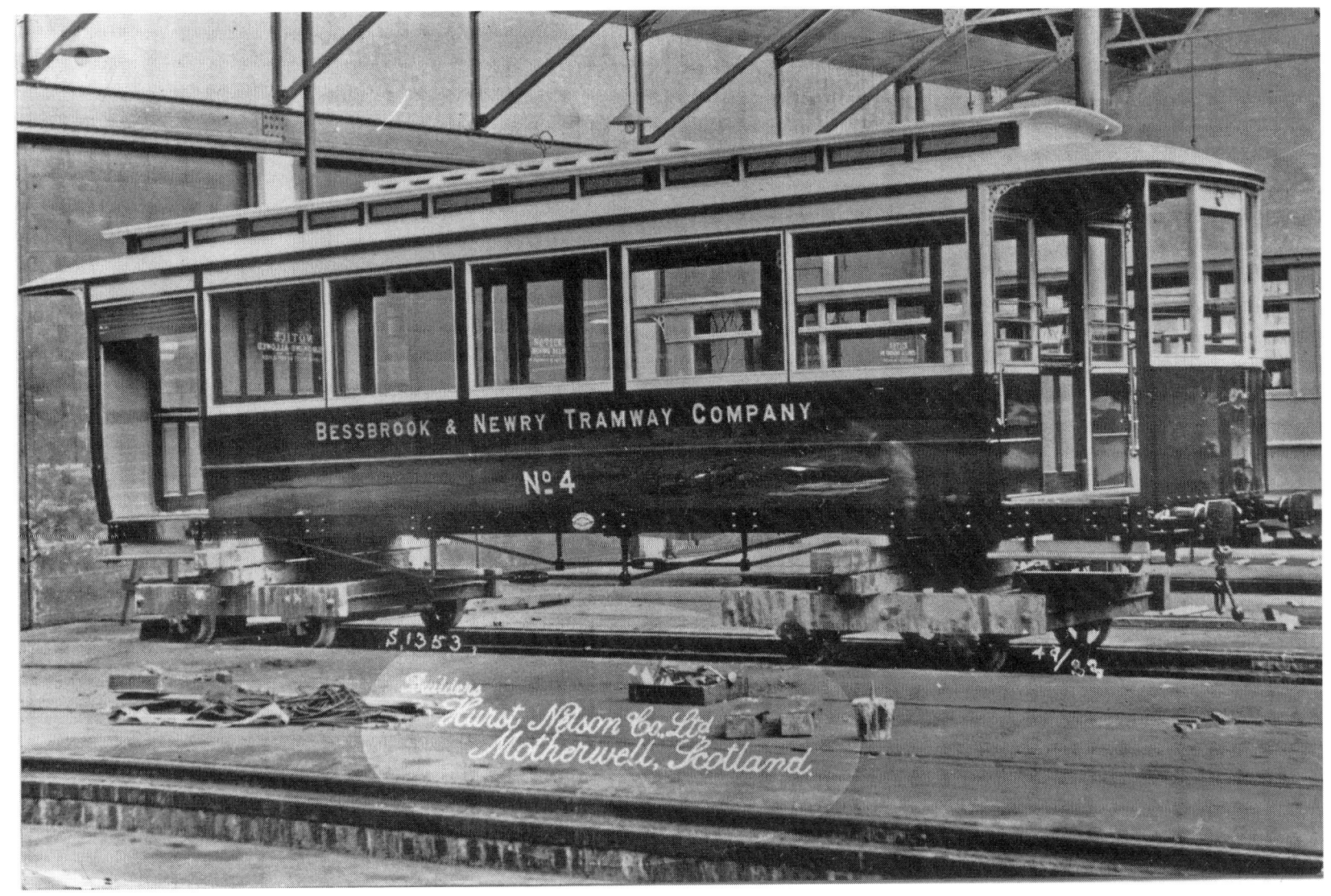

No. 4 car in the maker's works. At the left-hand side the roller shutter is raised allowing access to the luggage compartment.   *Hurst Nelson*

However, negotiations did not proceed smoothly, as the Government declined to bear the enhanced cost of the above items. Accordingly, on 17th May, the Directors decided to communicate with the Ministry of Transport, and threaten to close down the tramway if the authorities still refused to meet the above costs. The ultimatum apparently had good effect, as a more favourable attitude was shown by the Ministry, with the result that on 14th September, Messrs Hurst Nelson recorded orders for not merely one, but two cars, Nos. 1 and 4, No. 1 being a replacement for its predecessor, and No. 4 comprising a body and under frame for an additional vehicle (details of both will follow).

On 21st June, it was decided to ask Messrs James Wilson, of Warrenpoint, to quote for a new station building, also five platforms and walls at Newry. The reference to the latter is unexplainable, as there was never more than a single platform there; nevertheless this item comes from the company's Minutes. At some unknown period, a goods shed had been built in the centre of the loop, with two spurs leading to it. Repainting of the old station was to be abandoned, a contract having been given earlier for the repainting of Bessbrook, and Newry stations, also similar work at Millvale Crossing (possibly the Halt there).

To return to the new cars: No. 1 was 37 ft 1¾ in. over the buffers, having a body width of 6 ft 2 in.; height to trolley plank 11 ft; full length of wheelbase 29 ft 5 in., individual wheelbases measuring 4 ft. The body was divided into two compartments, with a sliding door, also similar glazed doors giving access to the platform. Longitudinal seating on each side of the car provided for 40 passengers. The roof was of clerestory type, with glazed ventilators, but the clerestory did not extend over the platforms, which had semi-circular dashes and windscreens. The bogies were of maximum-traction type (similar to tramway practice), with wheels of 30 in. and 20 in. diameter. One 36hp motor was fitted to each truck and the body had six windows each side.

No. 4 car was a composite, of similar dimensions, but had a luggage compartment, with side roller shutters reaching from roof to floor at one end, and in consequence of this, there was only accommodation for 32 passengers, and five windows each side. The usual sliding doors were provided, separating the two compartments, also doors giving access to the luggage compartment, and the other end, but only one motor of 25hp (Electric Construction Company (ECC), of Wolverhampton) was provided and a vestibuled platform at the driving end. The name of the undertaking appeared in small block letters, spread along the upper part of the side panels, with the car number positioned centrally lower down. In later years the number was moved up to follow the company's title. It was intended to use the old bogies from the original No. 1 car, but according to the late H. Fayle, this was not done.

Nevertheless, Mr J.C. Gillham, as a result of his investigations, considers that Car No. 4 was in fact, fitted with the trucks and motor of the original Car 1; the motor of the latter was, of course, only of 15hp, which with the ECC 25hp motor, would bring up the tractive power to 40hp. The bi-polar field of the old motor projected through the floor and thus could be probably accommodated in the luggage compartment, (unfortunately Minute Books for this period are not available). It would appear very unlikely that the body and underframe of Car No. 4 were bought merely for use as a spare unit. The fact remains that it was only in 1927 that Messrs Hurst, Nelson received an order for materials to reconstruct Car No. 4, comprising two 1118 Delta type motors of 22hp, one spare armature, one set of armature bearings, one set of axle bearings, also brake gear and materials to reconstruct the underframe at the opposite end, one controller, and two maximum traction trucks, and a windscreen for a platform at the altered (front) end; a platform and screen of course existed at the opposite end.

A further car, No. 5 (renumbered 7 about ten to fifteen years later) was also ordered from the same makers, on 27th September, 1920. This was a very small, open trailer car, mounted on a four-wheel goods type truck, having a composite steel and timber underframe, side spring buffers, screw couplings, and pitch-pine

Car No. 1 with a long train of wagons and car No. 6 as brakevan at Newry.

*Oakwood collection*

Car No. 5 the longitudinal seating can be seen through the access opening.

*H. Fayle*

longitudinal seating for 20 passengers. It was entirely devoid of windows and roof, the side panels only reaching to waist level. There was but one entrance, at the front end, where a tram-type handbrake was provided, and only a cross gangway. Where the company obtained the money to obtain cars 4 and 5 is unknown.

Another small car (No. 6) was delivered some time between 1922/24. This was fully enclosed with curved roof (non-clerestory), the passenger saloon being fully glazed with six windows per side, and three-pane windows each end. A full width entrance platform was provided at only one end, both ends being of flat format. The handbrake was of vertical railway type, and the general dimensions of the car were as follows: length 13 ft ½ in., width 5 ft 9 in. The seating (longitudinal and facing inwards) only accommodated 12 passengers, six per side. Its builders are unknown, but it was probably built locally; it would have been quite within the capabilities of any coach builder. On the other hand, it could have been built in Bessbrook Depot and the wheels obtained second-hand from the Great Northern Railway (Ireland), as there is no evidence of either Messrs Hurst Nelson, or Mather and Platt having received an order for it; again, the Minute Books, had they been available, could have cast light on this matter. (It should be mentioned that by 1920 the B&N had a stock of 27 wagons, of both open and closed types. For many years they had been hauled through the streets of Newry by horses, but later in the 20th century petrol tractors supplanted them.)

In 1928, two bogie single-deck trailers were acquired from the defunct Dublin & Lucan Electric Railway, which had become bankrupt, owing to intensive competition by privately-owned buses, on 29th January, 1925. Its assets were acquired by the Dublin United Tramways Company (1896) Ltd. who relaid and re-opened the line on its own 5 ft 3 in. gauge in May 1928. These cars dated back to the days of steam traction, when their line was of 3 ft gauge, but it had been relaid to 3 ft 6 in. gauge and re-opened with electric traction in 1899. This, of course, involved re-gauging the trucks to suit the Bessbrook lines 3 ft gauge track, either by obtaining new axles, or cutting the old ones to suit. As it is doubtful if Bessbrook shed had the equipment to undertake this task, it may be that the D.U.T. Co., or the Great Northern Railway (Ireland) had undertaken this work prior to delivery.

These cars ran for some time in their old Dublin & Lucan livery of green and pale cream, complete with the former garter crest, enclosing the serial number, on the side panels. Seating was longitudinal, comprising timber benches facing inwards, and the roof had high clerestories, with open ends.

These ex-Lucan cars were, however, of different lengths, No. 24 being the longer with nine windows per side, of equal width, and seated 26 passengers, 13 per side on longitudinal benches. Its general dimensions were as follows:- overall length 23 ft 5 in., body length 19 ft 2 in., width 5 ft 9 in., bogie wheelbase 18 ft 9 in. and wheel diameters 2 ft 4 in. On both cars the bogie trucks were positioned well forward, and partly under the platforms at each end, thus perpetuating steam tram practice.

No. 27 had eight windows per side, its overall dimensions being 20 ft 10 in., body length 15 ft 7 in., width 6 ft 3 in., total wheelbase 17 ft 9 in., and wheels 2 ft diameter. Seating accommodated 24 passengers, 12 each side, on longitudinal timber benches and, as on No. 24, these seats faced inwards. Eventually this car was repainted in its new owners' livery, with full title, followed by 'No. 5' in large black letters in the standard position along the upper part of the side panels. At this time the original Bessbrook and Newry four-wheeled car No. 5 was renumbered 7. It should be added that, when in Bessbrook and Newry service, this Lucan car had windows Nos. 1, 3, 5 and 7, from the leading to trailing ends on each side boarded up.

Some years later the original body of Bessbrook car No. 2 was removed and scrapped, and that of ex-Lucan No. 24, with one remaining platform and windscreen, substituted on its underframe. As this car was shorter than the body of No. 2, a luggage compartment, equal in length to two windows, was built in front of the passenger section. On one side a sliding door of vertical match-

Car No. 2 with ex-Dublin and Lucan trailers Nos. 27 and 24 behind it.

*W.J. Haynes*

No. 2 with its original body.

*H. Fayle*

No. 2 after its body had been replaced by that of ex-Dublin and Lucan Tramway No. 24.

*H. Fayle*

boarding was provided, being hung from overhead runners, the original roof of No. 24 being extended, and projected over No. 2's original platform and windscreen, which was retained, together with the controller, handbrake, dash and windscreen, this being carried on an extension from the underframe at the leading end. The roof extension was of flattish curvature square in front and, of course, non-clerestory. The luggage compartment still housed the original 1885 motor of No. 2, which it will be remembered, projected upwards through the floor. The original B&N tramway bogies were retained, together with coupling rods on the leading bogie. When this metamorphosis had been completed, the ex-Lucan body was painted in Bessbrook and Newry livery, with the title in full, followed by the number '2' on the upper side panels of the car.

This is a suitable place to refer to the spur from the rear of Bessbrook shed to a quarry, which was shown in the 1882 plans, and soon afterwards abandoned. A similar spur, but to an outlying mill, was however built later (date unknown) along a similar route. After emerging from the rear of Bessbrook shed, it crossed an adjacent roadway on the level, and then continued along a private right-of-way, curving right at the outer end. This section of line was paved in granite setts, similar to a street tramway, and only angle rails for guiding wagons were provided as distinct from the twin rails on the passenger section of the tramway, horse haulage of wagons being apparently the practice on this spur.

By the end of the Second World War, the tramway had become considerably run down, the track being overgrown, and there were gaps in the conductor rail, while the cars had become very slow, probably as a result of war conditions. The author can confirm the condition of the cars as he had in the course of a cycle tour in 1946, visited and travelled on the line. The cars were especially slow mounting the 1-in-50 gradient out of Newry, the conductor was devoid of a uniform, while his tickets, in roll form, were housed in a cylindrical aluminium box, having a hinged lid and slots for egress of tickets, shoulder straps being fitted to the box. As far as can, now be remembered there was not even a ticket punch. It should be added that by this time, the brick built shed and spurs leading thereto, in the centre of the Newry loop had been removed, a grass covered circular mound having replaced it. In the following Summer (1947) the Irish Railway Record Society, then in its infancy, paid an official visit to the tramway, the writer participating in this. By now, the 'writing on the wall' was plain respecting the not far distant demise of the undertaking, the Northern Ireland Road Transport Board having started a frequent bus service between Newry and Bessbrook. This being faster than the trams took away most of the passenger traffic therefrom.

It should be mentioned that a number of years earlier, the name of the undertaking on the sides of the cars had been curtailed: to the initial letters 'B.&N.Ty.Co.', followed by the car numbers, these being painted in large black letters in the same position.

Former Dublin & Lucan trailer No. 27 at Bessbrook on 16th August, 1938.
*E.W. Hannan*

The Bessbrook quarry spur line in 1965. *Author*

Bessbrook engine shed and terminal, 1965.

# The Tramway Closed

By October 1947 there were only eight journeys daily, and on 10th January, 1948 the line was closed. A staff member from the *Newry Reporter* was sent to ride on the last car, and had to admit that although he had lived in Newry all his life he had never ridden on the tramway. Only a few people attended, and he was the only one in the car by the time it reached Bessbrook. The conductor felt it was suitable to mention the old joke about the worker who was asked if he was going on the tram, and replied 'No I'm in a hurry today, I'll walk it.' It was the slow speed that made it an easy victim of bus competition; but then it had been designed in the days when the internal combustion engined heavy vehicle was 20 years in the future. It has not been possible to ascertain the name of the firm who undertook the demolition, but the author has definite confirmation that Messrs Thos. Ward & Co. of Sheffield (who did this work as regards the Listowel and Ballybunnion Railway) were not involved.

Messrs Mather and Platt, of Manchester, who built the original cars, re-purchased Car No. 2 and removed it to their factory at Newton Heath, near Manchester, where it was at first placed on wooden blocks on the side of their sports field as a cricket hut! Later it was moved to the factory yard and mounted on rails with access on one side comprising six steps with a square landing level with the car platform, whilst those at the driving end comprising simply four steps, as the car platform was on an extension from the bogie. The sliding door giving access to the luggage compartment and upper side of the drive to the motor was replaced with sliding doors having glass panels in the upper part. The car was then repainted with its full title on the side panels, but minus the number. This was later replaced with an oval plaque bearing the company title. The car remained here for a few years, then in the fifties, on the formation of the Belfast Transport Museum, under the aegis of the Belfast Museum and Art Gallery, it was returned to Ireland and along with other preserved exhibits was housed in the disused rail-motor depot of the County Down Railway near Queens Quay station, where it remained for some years; then a factory, formerly in use by Messrs James Mackie as a spinning mill, became vacant, and car No. 2, with the other exhibits, was moved to this new location in Witham Street, off the Newtownards Road, where it was placed on a length of rails in front of preserved Car No. 5 of the Giants Causeway Tramway. In 1967, the Belfast Transport Museum merged with the Folk Museum to form the Ulster Folk and Transport Museum. A new site for the transport museum has been provided near the Folk Museum's site on land adjoining Cultra station.

In the early summer of 1965, the author paid a return visit to the Bessbrook end of the former tramway, this time perforce by bus from Portadown to Newry and by local ones thence, the branch railway from Goraghwood having been closed. Bessbrook depot was still intact, although rather dilapidated, with advertisements on it, but the paved section of track on its own right of way to a mill, from the intervening roadway still existed. The intervening roadway had since been raised greatly, to ease the former sharp dip, and it may be that there is still a section of track underneath. The mini-platforms at the intervening Halts between Bessbrook and Millvale were still extant and it is understood that the similar Halt at Craigmore, between Millvale and Newry was in situ, but the former level crossing gates at Millvale had been replaced by an iron gate of full width. Moreover, the section of trackbed between here and Newry is still usable as a footpath.

Former Dublin & Lucan trailer still in its original livery, at Bessbrook.  *H. Fayle*

## Summary of Rolling Stock

| No. | Wheels | Class/Type | Length | Builder | Date |
|---|---|---|---|---|---|
| 1 | 8 | composite motored | 33 ft | Ashbury | 1885 |
| 2 | 8 | 2nd motored | 31 ft 5 in. | Starbuck | 1885 |
| 3 | 8 | 2nd trailer | 33 ft | Ashbury | 1885 |
| 4 | 8 | 2nd motored | 37 ft 1 in. | Hurst Nelson | 1921 |
| 5 | 4 | 2nd trailer | 13 ft 9 in. | Hurst Nelson | 1920 |
| 6 | 4 | 2nd trailer | 13 ft. | Hurst Nelson | 1922 |
| 7 | | | | see .No. 5 (renumbered) | |
| 1 | 8 | 2nd motored | 37 ft 1 in. | Hurst Nelson | 1921 |
| 5 | 8 | 2nd | 20 ft 10 in. | ex-Dublin & Lucan trailer No. 28 | purchased 1928 |

No. 2 rebodied with ex-Dublin & Lucan trailer No. 24, date unknown.

Example timetable of the tramway, date not known.   Oakwood collection

## Tickets

(Data from C. Gordon Stuart in Fayles' *Narrow-gauge Railways of Ireland*). Roll tickets (1932 onwards) the single tickets were mauve in colour, returns being yellow. Workers' weekly tickets: these measured approximately 2 5/16th by 3¼ in. They bore printed dates and were punched for each journey, whilst the holder was obliged to sign his name at the foot, a most unusual practice, and not in operation on any other line in the British Isles to Mr Stuart's knowledge. No class was shown on Workers' daily and weekly tickets. These fares were 1s. 3d. return from Bessbrook, and 8d. from Craigmore. The original ordinary tickets, bearing class, single or return and the company's title at top, in words, with the fare at foot, and serial numbers vertically at left side, were printed by Williamson of Ashton, Lanes., England, and 'issued subject to company's byelaws'. First class tickets were available until about 1921.

Barbrook Mill on 17th April, 1940; car No. 4 with van No. 2 and brake van No. 6.

W.A. Camwell